220

People of the Bible

The Bible through stories and pictures

Jesus Begins His Work

Jesus Begins His Work

Retold by Catherine Storr
Pictures by Chris Molan

Franklin Watts Limited · London
in association with Belitha Press Limited · London

Every year Mary and Joseph used to go
to Jerusalem for the feast of the Passover.
When Jesus was twelve years old,
he went with them.

When the feasting was over,
Mary and Joseph started
on the long journey back to Nazareth.
Jesus wasn't with them.

They thought he was travelling
with some other friends and relations.
It wasn't until the end of the first day
that they discovered he had been left behind.

Joseph and Mary had to go back to Jerusalem.
They looked everywhere for Jesus.
At last they found him in the Temple.
He was talking to the clever men there,
asking questions, and answering them too.

Mary said to him,
'How could you do this to us?
We've been terribly worried about you.'
Jesus said, 'Don't you know I have to do
what God tells me?'
But he went back to Nazareth with Joseph and Mary
and did what he was told.

Many years later, John the Baptist, a cousin of Jesus, was living in the wilderness.
He taught people to share their clothes and food with others, who were cold and hungry.
He said to them, 'I am not the greatest prophet.
But he is coming soon.
I have seen him and I know he is the son of God.'

One day, John was with two of his followers,
Andrew and Simon Peter.
He saw Jesus coming and he said to them,
'Look! There is the son of God.'

When Andrew heard this,
he left John and followed Jesus.
He said to his brother, Simon Peter,
'Come and see. We have found Christ, our leader.'
Jesus said, 'Follow me!'

Soon after this Jesus found Philip,
who followed him too.
As well as Andrew and Simon Peter and Philip,
there were James and John the sons of Zebedee,
Matthew and Bartholomew, Thomas and Simon,
James the son of Alphaeus, Thaddeus,
and Judas Iscariot.
All these men were called the disciples of Jesus.

One day there was a great wedding party
in a village called Cana.
Mary and Jesus and his disciples had all been invited.

But when they arrived at the feast,
all the wine had been drunk.

Mary said to Jesus, 'There's no more wine
for the guests to drink. Is there anything you can do?'
She said to the servants,
'Whatever my son tells you, you should do.'

Jesus told the servants to fill six great jars with water.
Then he said, 'Pour something to drink from the jars,
and take it to the master of the house.'
As they did this,
they saw that the water had turned into wine.
It was even better wine than they had drunk before.
This was Jesus' first miracle.

After this Jesus did many more miracles.
He made ill people better.
Once he was teaching in a house full of people,
and a man who couldn't stand or walk
was lowered on his bed through the roof
into the middle of the house.
Jesus said to him, 'Take up your bed and walk.'
The man found that he could do as he was told.
He was cured.

Another time, a blind man was brought to Jesus.
Jesus spat on some earth and rubbed it
on the man's eyes. Then he asked,
'What do you see?' The man said,
'I see men, like trees, but walking.'
He could see again.

One day, a ruler of the synagogue,
called Jairus, came to see Jesus and said,
'My little daughter is dying. Please save her.'
Jesus went to Jairus' house and found everyone there
crying and wailing. He said, 'Don't be sad.
The little girl isn't dead, she's only asleep.'
He went inside and took her by the hand and said,
'Get up!'
The little girl stood up, alive and well. Jesus said,
'Give her some food, and let's keep it a secret.'

Jesus and his disciples travelled to many places.
They took no money or food,
and taught people who came to listen to them.

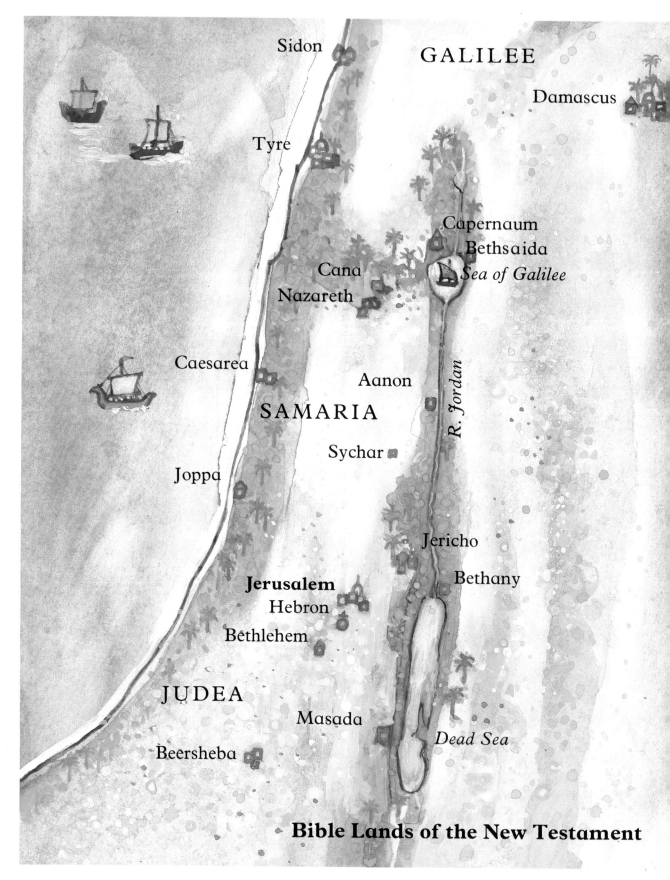

Sidon

GALILEE

Damascus

Tyre

Capernaum
Bethsaida
Sea of Galilee

Cana
Nazareth

Caesarea

Aanon

R. Jordan

SAMARIA

Sychar

Joppa

Jericho

Bethany

Jerusalem
Hebron
Bethlehem

JUDEA

Masada

Dead Sea

Beersheba

Bible Lands of the New Testament